Marbury v. Madison

The New Supreme Court Gets More Powers

Ryan P. Randolph

ROSEN CLASSROOM
PRIMARYSOURCE™

Rosen Classroom Books & Materials™
New York

Published in 2004 by The Rosen Publishing Group, Inc.
29 East 21st Street, New York, NY 10010

Library of Congress Cataloging-in-Publication Data

Randolph, Ryan P.
Marbury v. Madison: the new Supreme Court gets more powers / by Ryan Randolph.— 1st ed.
     p. cm. — (Life in the new American nation)
Summary: Examines the Supreme Court case of 1803 that marked the first time that a law passed by Congress was found to be illegal according to the Constitution.
Includes bibliographical references and index.
ISBN 0-8239-4034-9 (lib. bdg.)
ISBN 0-8239-4252-X (pbk. bdg.)
6-pack ISBN 0-8239-4265-1
1. Judicial review—United States—History—Juvenile literature. 2. Marbury, William, 1761 or 2–1835—Trials, litigation, etc.—Juvenile literature. 3. Madison, James, 1751–1836—Trials, litigation, etc.—Juvenile literature. [1. Judicial review—United States—History. 2. Marbury, William, 1761 or 2–1835—Trials, litigation, etc. 3. Madison, James, 1751–1836—Trials, litigation, etc.] I. Title. II. Series.
KF4575.Z9R36 2004
347.73'12—dc21

                                                                          2002154615

Manufactured in the United States of America

Cover (left): James Madison
Cover (right): William Marbury

Photo credits: cover (left) Independence National Historical Park; cover (right), p. 6 Collection of the Supreme Court of the United States; p. 1 National Archives and Records Administration; pp. 5, 12 © Hulton/Archive/Getty Images; pp. 9, 17 © AP/Wide World Photos; p. 10 © Scala/Art Resource, NY; p. 15 General Records of the United States Government, National Archives and Records Administration; p. 20 © National Portrait Gallery, Smithsonian Institution/Art Resource, NY; p. 22 Records of the Supreme Court of the United States, National Archives and Records Administration; p. 26 Library of Congress Prints and Photographs Division.

Designer: Nelson Sá; Editor: Eliza Berkowitz; Photo Researcher: Amy Feinberg

Contents

Introduction

Marbury v. Madison is the name of a court case that was decided by the Supreme Court of the United States in 1803. Marbury and Madison were two people who went to court over a disagreement. This disagreement had a big impact on the United States government. *Marbury v. Madison* was important because it gave the Supreme Court a larger role in the government of the United States.

The case of *Marbury v. Madison* was ruled on by the Supreme Court. The Supreme Court is the highest court in the United States. The court system judges if people and groups are following the laws. This case marked the first time the Supreme Court ruled that a law passed by Congress was illegal according to the Constitution. This concept is known as judicial review. In other words, the Supreme Court used its power of judicial review to say that a law passed by Congress was not constitutional.

At the time of *Marbury v. Madison*, the Supreme Court had six judges. These judges were also called justices. Today, there are nine justices. The president of the United States appoints a Supreme Court justice for life. The Senate must approve the choice. Justices can leave the Court only if they retire or are guilty of a crime. The head of the Supreme Court is known as the chief justice. At the time of *Marbury v. Madison*, John Marshall was the chief justice. John Marshall served in this position for thirty-four years. He was the chief justice from 1801 to 1835.

James Madison was the fourth president of the United States. Madison was the defendant in the *Marbury v. Madison* court case. Although he was the defendant in this court case, he never went before the Supreme Court.

These are the six Supreme Court justices that served during the *Marbury v. Madison* court case. They are *(clockwise from top left)* Alfred Moore, William Cushing, William Paterson, Samuel Chase, Bushrod Washington, and John Marshall.

Three people served as chief justice before John Marshall. They each served for a very short amount of time. Back then, the Supreme Court was not a key part of the government. In fact, John Marshall was appointed chief justice while also serving as the secretary of state to the president! His job was considered easy enough for him to take on another role in the government.

Today, a Supreme Court justice holds a very important job. John Marshall shaped the direction of the Supreme Court. He made the Supreme Court a more powerful part of the government.

Plaintiff v. Defendant

Court cases are named using the people or groups on each side of the argument. The first name in the title of a case is known as the plaintiff. The plaintiff is the person or group with a complaint that starts a court case. The second name is the defendant, or the person or group that defends against the complaint. In the case of *Marbury v. Madison*, William Marbury was the plaintiff. The secretary of state, James Madison, was the defendant.

Chapter 1

The Politics Behind the Case

The case of *Marbury v. Madison* had a big impact on U.S. history. John Marshall did not know that his decision in the case would be so big. The case was important to Marshall because of the politics of his time.

When George Washington became the first president, there were no political parties. A political party is a group of people who have similar ideas on how to best run a country. People vote for leaders that are part of a political party that best matches the ideas they believe in. During the start of the United States, people worked together to set up the new nation. They did not divide into groups. Washington led the United

This painting was created by Ramon de Elorriaga in 1889. It is entitled *The Inauguration of George Washington*. Washington's inauguration is significant because he was the first president to be sworn into office in the United States. The ceremony was conducted on April 30, 1789, in New York City. New York was then the U.S. capital.

States to freedom in the American Revolution. Nobody wanted to go against Washington's wishes, because he was greatly admired for his help in the Revolution. When Washington retired after eight years as president, two political parties had formed.

Today, the Democrats and the Republicans are the two largest political parties. Two early U.S. political parties were the Democratic-Republicans and the Federalists. The Democratic-Republicans were also known as Jeffersonian Republicans. They were different from the Republican Party of today. Thomas Jefferson and James Madison were leaders of this party. In general, farmers and landowners supported the Jeffersonian Republicans. Republicans believed that the United States would gain wealth through farming. Many people in the southern states, like Virginia, were Republicans because they had farms and owned land.

This is a color lithograph of a plantation on the Mississippi. Plantations were places where large amounts of crops were grown. Many southerners owned farms like these and believed that farming would make the United States wealthy.

Republicans also did not want the government to spend and borrow large amounts of money. They wanted each state government to remain powerful. They did not want the federal government to be stronger than the states.

In contrast, the Federalists wanted the federal government to be strong. Leaving power to the states would make it too hard to remain a union. Federalists wanted the national government to borrow and spend money. They felt that this would help businesses in the United States grow. Federalists believed supporting businesses would help the nation become strong and independent.

Many people in the northern states were Federalists because they were merchants. Alexander

Thomas Jefferson was a key founding father of the United States. He was also a well-known political leader who became the third president of the United States in 1801. In 1776, he wrote the Declaration of Independence. In this famous document, the United States declared freedom from Great Britain. Jefferson founded the University of Virginia. He was also one of the leaders of the Democratic-Republicans, also called the Jeffersonian Republicans.

John Adams was a Federalist. During his time as president of the United States, he made sure that there were many Federalists in office. He wanted to make sure that Federalist ideas were carried out by the government.

Hamilton and John Adams led the Federalists. John Adams was elected the second president of the United States.

John Marshall was also a Federalist. Marshall was the secretary of state and a close adviser to John Adams. Marshall started his career as a lawyer. He represented the United States in France after the Revolutionary War. He had also represented Virginia in Congress.

When John Adams was president, it meant the Federalists were in charge of running the country. Federalists also made up most of Congress. The Federalists made laws that matched their ideas on how best to run the United States.

The Republicans did not agree with many of these policies and laws. They wanted the people to vote for Republicans in the next elections.

Chapter 2

Marbury v. Madison Goes to Court

In 1801, John Adams lost the presidential election to Thomas Jefferson. Many Republicans were also elected to Congress. This meant Republicans could now make their own laws. Jefferson became president in March 1801.

The Constitution created the federal court system but did not give details on how to create new courts. The Judiciary Act of 1789 was a law that created rules for the courts. It was the job of the president and Congress to appoint new judges. Federalist leaders appointed people who held the same beliefs as them to be judges.

Judges were not elected. Federalists could still control the courts after they left office if they had

This is the federal Judiciary Act of 1789. This act created a federal court system for the United States. The judges appointed to the courts were picked by the people in power. Because of this, most of the people in government were all members of the same political party and held the same beliefs.

William Marbury was at the center of the *Marbury v. Madison* case. He was born in Maryland in 1762. He was involved in finance and became a powerful member of Maryland's government. Marbury supported the Federalist Party. He was able to become wealthy because of the complicated financial policies the Federalists used. Marbury was also friends with key Federalist leaders in Annapolis, Maryland.

appointed Federalist judges. In early 1801, Federalists made a law that created even more positions for judges. The Judiciary Act of 1801 was passed before Adams left office. Adams appointed several of his supporters to be new judges. John Marshall was the secretary of state to Adams. He helped make the appointments official.

The Marbury in the case of *Marbury v. Madison* was William Marbury. He was appointed to be a justice of the peace in Washington, D.C. A justice of the peace is a type of judge. They handle small legal matters in local areas around the country.

Adams was still appointing judges during his last day in office. In the rush of leaving, the stamped papers (also called commissions) that allowed Marbury to become a judge never got delivered.

Thomas Jefferson was elected to be president after Adams. Jefferson was a Republican. He did not want more Federalist judges. Jefferson knew he would cause a political crisis if he did not let any of the judges receive the commissions Adams had given them when he was still in office.

This portrait of Thomas Jefferson was made in 1786 by Mather Brown. Jefferson was the third president of the United States. He was also a Republican and wanted to have other Republicans in power, unlike the way it was when the Federalists were in control.

Jefferson decided to let most of the commissions get delivered but not those that were for strong Federalist supporters. It is likely that Jefferson told James Madison not to give the commission to Marbury. He would have done this because Marbury was considered a big Federalist supporter.

James Madison was the secretary of state for Jefferson. The secretary of state is part of the cabinet of the president. One thing the secretary of state's office was in charge of was delivering commissions.

Marbury knew that he had been appointed a judge, but he had never received his commission. He didn't understand why his commission had not been delivered. To his Federalist friends, it seemed like the Republicans were breaking the law. They knew that Jefferson had prevented the new Federalist judges from receiving their commissions. Marbury and the Federalists brought the case to the Supreme Court.

The Decision by John Marshall

Madison's office did not give the commission to Marbury and other judges. The Republicans said the commissions were not official because they were not delivered. They argued this meant Marbury was never officially appointed to be a judge.

Marbury's lawyer was a Federalist named Charles Lee. He argued that the commission was official. It was the duty of the new secretary of state to deliver it. Lee demanded that the commission be delivered. He requested that the Supreme Court issue a document known as a writ of mandamus.

A writ of mandamus is a legal term for a document from a court ordering an official duty to be

Alonzo Chappel painted this picture of John Marshall, the chief justice of the Supreme Court from 1801 to 1835. During Marshall's term as chief justice, he helped the Supreme Court get more powers.

done. In other words, the writ of mandamus would force Madison to give the commission to Marbury.

The case of *Marbury v. Madison* put the Supreme Court in a tough spot. The court was in a showdown with the Republican president and Congress. John Marshall and the other five justices were Federalists.

They thought that Marbury should receive his commission. Marshall himself had sealed the commission. If the Supreme Court said that Marbury was right, it would have to issue the order to deliver the commission to Marbury. Marshall knew that Jefferson would ignore the order from the Court. If the president ignored the order, the Supreme Court would be seen as weak. Marshall wanted to avoid this. He also believed in a strong role for the Supreme Court and did not want the decision to be ignored.

Marshall thought about the case and wrote his decision. The other five justices agreed with the decision. He wrote that Marbury should be given his commission, but the Supreme Court could not rule on the case.

Marshall started by saying that Marbury should be given the commission to be a judge. The commission was Marbury's legal right, and Madison and Jefferson

This is John Marshall's decision in the *Marbury v. Madison* case. This document explains why the Supreme Court would not rule on this case. Interestingly, the document bears marks from the Capitol fire of 1898.

should give it to him. Marshall went on to say that a writ of mandamus was the correct legal action for Marbury to seek against Madison.

The complex part is that Marshall said that the Supreme Court could not issue the writ of mandamus. Marshall said the Constitution did not give the Supreme Court the power to issue the writ. However, the Judiciary Act of 1789 passed by Congress gave the Supreme Court the power. Marshall wrote that the law that Congress had passed was illegal because it was not allowed in the Constitution.

The Constitution is the original, top law of the United States. If Congress or a state government made a law in conflict of the Constitution, the law was not valid. It would be unconstitutional. It was up to the Supreme Court to decide if a law was unconstitutional. This was called judicial review.

In the short term, Marbury did not win his case and the Republicans won. Marshall also avoided a conflict with the president. In the long term, the Supreme Court became more important. Marshall's decision gave the Court more power. With judicial review, the Supreme Court could strike down laws passed by Congress.

Chapter 4

The Legacy of
Marbury v. Madison

Marshall said the Supreme Court had the right of judicial review according to the Constitution. It is interesting to note that in the Constitution, it does not say that the Supreme Court can declare laws unconstitutional or not. John Marshall interpreted the meaning of the Constitution to say that the Supreme Court could.

Marshall concluded that the Constitution had to allow for judicial review so that the Supreme Court could be as powerful as Congress and the president. He believed it was necessary to keep the federal government strong. At the time, nobody, not even Jefferson, fought against

Marshall's claim that the Supreme Court had the right of judicial review.

During the time John Marshall was the chief justice, the Court did not use judicial review in many cases. The Supreme Court tried to stay out of decisions that were political.

Some people question whether judicial review was right. The people do not elect the Supreme Court. The people elect Congress and state governments. Congress makes laws most people support or they risk not being elected again. Judicial review meant that a few judges could declare laws illegal that were passed by Congress, which is elected by many.

Today, most would say that the Supreme Court has used judicial review to make good and bad decisions in history. Many decisions depend on the beliefs of the justices on the Supreme Court. They also depend on the political situation of the time.

One example of a bad decision was *Scott v. Sanford* in 1857. In the case, an African American named Dred Scott was seeking freedom in the Supreme Court. The Court ruled that Dred Scott was not free. The Court

This is a newspaper article from 1857, published in *Frank Leslie's Illustrated Newspaper*. It is the front-page story of the Dred Scott decision of 1857 and features illustrations of Scott and his family.

decided a law in Congress that made African Americans free in some states was illegal.

Another example of a bad decision by the Supreme Court was *Plessy v. Ferguson* in 1896. The Supreme Court ruled that laws allowing segregation were legal. They ruled that black people and white people could be legally separated as long as they were equal. They interpreted the Constitution to mean that segregation laws were legal because the Constitution did not say segregation was not allowed.

In the twentieth century, the Supreme Court made some good decisions. In the 1954 case of *Brown v. Board of Education*, the Supreme Court ruled that segregation laws were illegal. The justices did not look back to the *Plessy v. Ferguson* case. They interpreted the Constitution in a different way that did not allow for segregation.

Judicial review was used to protect the freedoms of speech and religion that the Constitution provides all Americans. Today, the idea that the judge can be a powerful force in government has spread. Many other countries have a powerful judicial branch to watch over the laws passed by the political leaders.

Glossary

appointment (ah-POINT-ment) A position or office held without election.

commission (ko-MISH-on) An official document giving power to perform a job.

Constitution (kon-STI-too-shen) The written document ratified in 1788 that set the basic laws, powers, and duties of the United States.

defendant (de-FEN-dent) The person or group that answers a legal complaint against them.

federal government (FEH-duh-ruhl GOV-ehrn-ment) The national government of the United States.

Federalist (FEH-duh-ruh-list) A member of a major political party in the early years of the United States favoring a strong, centralized, national government.

interpret (in-TER-priht) To explain or tell the meaning of.

judicial (ju-DISH-el) The branch of government

that hears court cases that involve the government or are in the court's area.

judicial review (ju-DISH-el ri-VYOO) The right of a court system to void or cancel laws that judges find unconstitutional.

merchant (MER-chent) A person that buys or sells items to make money; a person who runs a business.

plaintiff (PLAYN-tif) The person or group with a complaint that starts a court case.

Republican (rih-PUH-blih-ken) A member of a political party in the early United States associated with farming and land interests that favored a restricted role for national government.

segregation (seg-ri-GAY-shun) The social and physical separation of black and white people in America.

unconstitutional (un-kon-sti-TOO-shuh-nul) Not according to or consistent with the constitution of a nation.

writ of mandamus (RIT of man-DAH-mus) A court order for an official duty to be done.

Web Sites

Due to the changing nature of Internet links, the Rosen Publishing Group, Inc., has developed an online list of Web sites related to the subject of this book. This site is updated regularly. Please use this link to access the list:

http://www.rosenlinks.com/lnan/mavm

Primary Source Image List

Page 6: (*left to right, top row*) 1. Official portrait of Justice William Cushing by artist C. Gregory Stapko 2. Official portrait of Justice Alfred Moore by artist C. Gregory Stapko 3. Official portrait of Justice William Patterson by artist C. Gregory Stapko (*left to right, bottom row*) 1. Portrait of Chief Justice John Marshall by artist John B. Martin 2. Official portrait of Justice Bushrod Washington by artist Adrian Lamb 3. Official Portrait of Justice Samuel Chase by artist Larry Dodd Wheeler. All paintings photographed by Vic Boswell. All are housed in the collection of the Supreme Court of the United States, Office of the Curator.
Page 9: Painting entitled *The Inauguration of George Washington*. Created in 1889 by Ramon de Elorriaga.
Page 10: Color lithograph from the nineteenth century. Housed in the Museum of the City of New York.
Page 15: The federal Judiciary Act from 1789. Housed in the General Records of the United States government, Record Group 11, National Archives.
Page 17: Portrait of Thomas Jefferson by Mather Brown. Created in 1786.
Page 20: This is an oil on canvas painting of John Marshall by William James Hubard. Created in 1832. Housed in the collection of the National Portrait Gallery, Smithsonian Institution.
Page 22: The 1803 decision in the *Marbury v. Madison* court case. Housed in the Records of the Supreme Court of the United States, Record Group 267, National Archives.
Page 26: Front page of *Frank Leslie's Illustrated Newspaper* from 1857. Photos show (*top*) Eliza and Lizzie, children of Dred Scott, and (*bottom*) Dred Scott and Harriet, his wife. Housed in the Library of Congress, Prints and Photographs Division.

Index

About the Author

Ryan P. Randolph is a freelance writer with an interest in history. Ryan has a bachelor of arts degree in both history and political science from Colgate University in Hamilton, New York. He has written several history books for children. He currently works for a consulting firm and lives with his wife in Mount Vernon, New York.